Magic MOMENTS

*A Busy Woman's Guide
to Forgotten Pleasures*

by
Kim Goad

Happy Birthday!

*To Irene ~
Treat yourself
to a magic
moment!

Kim Goad
2/98*

Commune-a-Key Publishing
Salt Lake City, Utah

Commune-a-Key Publishing
P.O. Box 58637
Salt Lake City, UT 84158
(801) 581-9191
(801) 581-9196 Fax

Library of Congress Cataloging-in-Publication Data
Goad, Kim, 1966–
    Magic moments : a busy woman's guide to forgotten pleasures / by Kim Goad.
    p. cm.
    ISBN: 1-881394-10-7 (pbk.: alk. paper)
    1. Women—Psychology—Miscellanea. 2. Self-realization—Miscellanea.
    I. Title.
    HQ1206.G66 1997
    158.1'082—dc21   97-12432
                                                  CIP

$9.95 U.S. – Prices may vary outside the U.S.

Editorial: Caryn Summers
Cover Design: Lightbourne Images, Ashland, OR
Typeset Design & Graphics: Bailey-Montague & Associates, Salt Lake City, UT
Photography: Robert Smith, Baltimore, MD

To Steve and Sandy,
my most dedicated coaches
and biggest fans.

Acknowledgments

I did not magically pull this book out of a hat—but there were many magical people who helped me bring it to life. My heartfelt appreciation goes to:

Steve, my wonderful husband, who supported and encouraged me every step of the way along this magnificent journey. Thank you for giving me the priceless gift of your love.

Sandy Reusing, my best friend and creative partner, whose strokes of genius helped me to create a work of which I am truly proud. Thanks for, well, just everything.

All of the busy women who added strength and authenticity to this book through their personal stories and ideas. Thank you for your powerful insights and for so willingly contributing to this project.

Mary Branning, my compass, who provided my initial direction and guidance in this quest. Thanks for listening—but also for hearing.

Caryn Summers and Nancy Lang, my enthusiastic publisher and editors, who allowed me to share my ideas with the world. Thank you for making my words sparkle, for pulling this project together in such a short period of time, and for being so downright nice.

Dot Sparer, my mentor and friend, who taught me so much about writing—and living. Thank you for bringing out the best in me.

My friends and family who lifted me up and allowed me to cross the finish line. Thanks, especially, to my mother and father for raising me to believe that I could do anything. As usual, you were right!

Table of Contents

Preface

"Life isn't a matter of milestones, but of moments."
— *Rose Fitzgerald Kennedy*

Do you believe in magic? I think in the truest sense of the word, we all do. Magic touches our lives every day and comes in many forms. The welcome song of a robin on the first day of spring. A well deserved vacation. The innocent delight in a baby's smile. A long hug from your best friend. The triumph of a job well done. They're all magic moments—events, actions, pastimes—anything that touches your soul, creates a smile, sparks motivation, or helps you savor the pleasures of everyday living.

For busy women like us, too often the demands of career, family, and community monopolize our time and control our schedules—sometimes willingly, sometimes because we just don't feel like fighting anymore. The good news is we really don't have to fight to find time for the things we enjoy—time to savor life's magic moments and to actively create magic moments of our own. That time is already there. But we must slow down long enough to let our hearts and minds tell us how to use it to its greatest and most joyful potential. It's not easy, but I know it's possible.

After seven years of working in a variety of professional positions in corporations and non-profit organizations, I began my search for life's magic moments by striking out on my own. I started a home-based publishing company—writing and producing small publications like newsletters, magazines and brochures. I thought it would be a dream come true. I could wear my pajamas to work, set my own hours, take as much vacation time as I wanted, and work in the office with my dog. But I quickly became disenchanted with this fairy tale. Although I was able to do some of these things, I really didn't allow myself to take full advantage of this new-found freedom. Instead, I let the business take over my life.

My hard work did not come without its own rewards. I received rave reviews for my services and boasted an ever-growing client roster. Although my company was successful by many standards, I felt passionless about my work. I was burnt-out and dissatisfied. I was working longer hours than ever before. I found that "being your own boss" is one of the myths of business ownership. Not only did I have to answer to myself, but to my 20 or so clients—each, in essence, one of many bosses. To myself, I was not a true example of success. I had let myself down.

After more than a year of deadlines, doldrums, and dilemmas, I began to realize that I could take greater control of the situation. I was in charge of my destiny, for whom I worked, and of which projects I took on. I didn't necessarily buck the system, rather, I found a way to work within it on my own terms. I began referring some potential clients to other capable associates. I turned down work when I was already swamped. I stopped working by 6 p.m. or earlier every week night, and put a halt to working on weekends. I began to accept or initiate only those projects that I enjoyed. I scheduled no meetings on Fridays. And, I took frequent breaks to refresh my body and soul. Most important, I allowed my values to guide me—not those imposed by society-at-large, like wealth, power, and the traditional definition of success. As a result, I felt closer to my true destiny because I was creating a more fulfilling life.

Make no mistake—I wasn't any less busy. On the contrary, I was doing more things that energized me and surrounded my home and me with beauty and inspiration. In essence, I used my new-found time to rediscover the magic in my life. I pursued other interests with zeal—biking, strength training, reading, singing, cooking, public speaking and working actively with community organizations. Even the simplest activities were revitalizing: gazing at a sky full of stars, picking a bouquet of spring flowers from my backyard, or playing fetch with my dog. The results of this shift in philosophy were life-changing. So much so that I decided to write this book to share my experiences with other busy women who so often get swept away in the whirlwind of productivity, power, and other people's expectations.

In January, 1996, I started the new year with a one-month, solitary retreat to the beaches of South Carolina. Away from the constraints of home, work, husband, pets, and my other responsibilities, I was free to create every day from scratch. I flourished on my own and savored every minute. I spent my time organizing ideas for this book, journaling, brainstorming new business ideas, sightseeing, trying new recipes, strolling along the beach in search of shells, and watching sunset after glorious sunset. Check-out time came all too soon, but I left with a renewed sense of self and a greater understanding of my true priorities.

When I returned home, my attitude didn't dwindle, as it often did after a shorter vacation. It thrived and set the standards for the way I now operate my business and live my life. In fact, "living" is now the priority, and work is included as one of the many parts of my life that makes me whole. I may not be wealthy, powerful, or famous, but in many ways, I'm richer than ever before. I'm much happier and content because I'm able to enjoy ordinary pleasures—those magic moments—that I once overlooked or took for granted.

To get you started on the road to greater fulfillment, I've filled this book with ideas—large and small, quick and time-consuming, trite and triumphant—that will help you uncover forgotten pleasures. They're ideas that add magic to all areas of your life—from how you spend your private time to the foods you eat. These magic moments can be things that inspire you, lift your spirits, energize you, foster comraderie, spark romance, or boost your image. You can do them by yourself or by enlisting the companionship of family and friends. By incorporating just a few of these simple ideas into your routine, you'll find that you begin to make them a priority. Soon, you'll be creating more time for magic moments because they've become so important and so fulfilling. You'll also find that you'll become a better, more balanced person as a result—much more capable of meeting and enjoying all of your other responsibilities.

To help me prove that there's still hope for personal renewal in these days of faxes, cellular phones, modems and instant gratification, I've enlisted the help of "some of America's busiest women" who share their secrets of relaxation and rejuvenation throughout this book in segments called "Busy Woman's Break." These women are authors and athletes, entrepreneurs and professionals, educators and politicians, single working moms and VIPs. Their examples and ideas show that even the busiest of women are committed to refueling their own spirits. And in most cases, this commitment is a large part of their success and contentment.

These women are also part of a quiet revolution that's taking place in America. It's about redefining success and making your life whole by infusing work, family, community and play into one cohesive unit—yourself. It's about choosing to do the things that bring the greatest joy. Although these things are different for every person, they all achieve the same result—greater personal and professional fulfillment. And often, because we're doing the things we love, financial gains follow—regardless of whether or not they are our primary goal.

Join me now for a journey of personal discovery—regardless of your age, job title, or lot in life. This book can help any woman make positive changes that enhance her life with joy and grace. To allow room for original thoughts, I've included a blank page at the end of each chapter for you to record your own magic moments. I hope that in the days, months, and years to come you will continue to refer to this book whenever you feel the need to leap out of the rut and refresh your belief in magic!

PART 1

Instant Exhilarators
Firing up the body and soul

"Life is either a daring adventure or nothing."
– Helen Keller

Need a quick pick-me-up to revive your mind, body and soul? Instead of letting the hustle and bustle of your daily life wear you down, try these refreshing ideas for quick rejuvenation. Go ahead—I dare you!

*V*olunteer for a community organization that supports a cause you believe in.

♦

Share a good feeling or accomplishment with a friend or loved one.

$\mathscr{C}$heck in on your child while he or she is sleeping.

✦

Stand up straight and exude confidence.

✦

Open the blinds and let the sun shine in!

Go polar-bearing. Put on your bathing suit and jump into a cold lake, ocean, river or swimming pool just after the crack of dawn.

♦

Try something daring—anything that requires personal courage. For some, it might be skydiving, for others, it might simply be saying "I love you."

$\mathcal{B}$uy yourself a beautiful piece of jewelry—whatever you can afford. You deserve it!

◆

Pause between activities. A deep breath or a quick stretch can help prepare you for your next challenge.

Make a "joy box" full of things that make you smile. What to include? How about:

+ A favorite photo or cartoon.
+ A pair of Groucho glasses.
+ Scented hand lotion.
+ Flower seeds.
+ A hilarious, old driver's license photo.
+ Hot cocoa mix.
+ Bubble gum.
+ A letter of commendation.

$\mathcal{G}$et movin'. Take a brisk walk.

◆

Drink a tall glass of ice water.

◆

Laugh out loud!

$\mathcal{S}$ay goodbye to junk.

- ✦ Clean out your closets and drawers and donate old or unworn clothes to charity.
- ✦ Clear the cobwebs out of the attic. Go through old boxes to uncover lost treasures and bury the old junk.
- ✦ Organize the files in your desk. Store the ones that are more than a year old, and throw out the catalogs, memos and mailers you haven't looked at more than once—and will most likely never look at again.
- ✦ Clean out your wallet. Discard expired coupons, cut up extra credit cards, and replace five-year-old pictures with the latest family photos.

$\mathcal{H}$ave a "quickie" with your partner.

✦

Put your favorite song on the stereo
and belt it out!

✦

Light a scented candle.

Take five. Research has shown that people who take five-minute breaks every hour are more productive than those who work straight through.

◆

Every morning, open a door or window and take in a deep breath of fresh air.

$\mathcal{L}$et out a long sigh.

◆

Soak your feet in hot water.

◆

Go braless!

*P*ractice common courtesy:

- ◆ Hold the door open for the person behind you.
- ◆ Let someone cut in front of you in line.
- ◆ Allow a car to merge onto the highway.
- ◆ Share your umbrella on a rainy day.
- ◆ Use your turn signal.
- ◆ Split the lunch check in half, even though you had less to eat than your friend or colleague.
- ◆ Say "please" and "thank you."

$\mathcal{R}$ide a rollercoaster.

✦

Take a cold shower.

✦

Experience a moment of blessed silence.

$\mathcal{R}$ead the infamous editorial, "Is There a Santa Claus?" It's a hopeful commentary written especially for Virginia at Christmas, but one that applies to all of us any time of year. You can find it at your local library in the *American Book of Days*.

Slip on a wacky pair of underwear. My favorite is yellow with a big smiley face on the front and back.

✦

Blast the radio in your car and sing along to your favorite song. (When other drivers see you gettin' down, they won't be able to resist smiling!)

Busy Woman's Break

Like many women, Marguerite Lykes spends much of her time taking care of others. As a single mother of two, she strives to keep up with her children's active lifestyles. And as spa director at the world-famous **Broadmoor Resort** in Colorado Springs, she aims to meet the needs of hotel guests.

Fortunately, her job does have relaxing perks. "For my own rejuvenation and to test the quality of massage therapists we hire at the spa, I try to get a massage every week," she explains. "Aromatherapy massage is probably one of the most relaxing things anyone can do. Time becomes a non-entity, and you're able to just let go."

Marguerite's other responsibilities include serving on the board of a spa in California and volunteering as a Junior Achievement consultant. She says, "If I don't set aside a little time to take care of myself, I'd just disappear. All of my energy and spirit would be going out, and nothing would be coming in."

$\mathscr{B}$usy Woman's Break

"I love to work, but I think it's important to have some non-work things I'm passionate about," says Doris Meister, managing director for **Copley Real Estate Advisors** in Boston and a board member of several non-profit organizations.

"When I want to recharge my batteries, I need things that offer me the same intensity and focus—things I truly love doing, like attending cultural activities and shopping for art and antiques. To alleviate stress and stay healthy, I exercise every day—outside whenever possible."

✦ Your Instant Exhilarators ✦

PART 2

Private Treasures
Creating sweet solitudes

"What a commentary on our civilization, when being alone is considered suspect; when one has to apologize for it, make excuses, hide the fact that one practices it—like a secret vice."

— Anne Morrow Lindbergh

The phone rings. Your boss hands you another deadline. The TV blares out the evening news. The kids yell out, "Mom," for the millionth time. To prepare you for the onslaught of endless demands, it's vital to find private time to regroup, revitalize, and refocus. These suggestions open the doors of your soul to a host of solitary pleasures.

*P*ractice before-bed rituals that help you relax or lull you to sleep. Read romantic novels or poetry, pray, or listen to soothing music.

◆

Try some solo sports, like a round of mini-golf, rollerblading, skiing, ice skating, walking or at-home aerobics.

$\mathcal{F}$ind a special place that refreshes and inspires you—whether it's the swing set in a nearby playground or a rock perched on top of a hill. Use it as a regular retreat to reflect, read, or watch the wind blow through the flowers.

Keep a journal, entering your thoughts every day, every week, or whenever the mood strikes. It's amazing how writing things down can help you rekindle wonderful moments, put things in perspective, and even help you solve problems.

Take a warm, scented bath by candlelight. (A glass of good wine is an optional, but exceptional, addition.)

◆

Spend quality time with your pet, whether it's playing, walking, grooming, or cuddling.

*I*ndulge in the beauty of the outdoors. By focusing on the miracles of mother nature, we're able to forget our worries and concentrate on our goals and dreams.

- ✦ Watch as the sun sets on the horizon.
- ✦ Sit outside on your porch during a thunderstorm.
- ✦ Watch birds making a nest.
- ✦ Smell the roses, lilacs, honeysuckle, or whichever fragrant flowers are in season.
- ✦ Listen to the wind blowing through the trees.

$\mathcal{W}$rite a "love letter" to your mate, mother, father, best friend, or pet—anyone who has touched your life in a positive way. Send it or just keep it tucked away in your journal as a reminder of how much this person (or creature) means to you.

◆

Take a nostalgic look at treasured mementos—old yearbooks, love letters, report cards, and grade school class pictures.

29

*E*scape from the "unreal" world. Go an entire day without turning on the TV.

◆

Take a country drive on a sunny day.

◆

Lie in a hammock with a good book and a glass of lemonade.

$\mathcal{D}$o something special for yourself on your birthday. Create a solitary ritual that invigorates you for the year to come.

+ Bake yourself a cake.
+ Get a massage.
+ Go out to lunch.
+ Write a list of the reasons you are thankful to be alive. Make the list as long as your years of age.

Rock yourself to serenity on the porch as you watch the neighborhood bustle by.

◆

Go on a vacation by yourself—even if it's only for a few days. You may like it so much that you'll decide to do it every year.

There's a new holiday on the horizon that's especially for you—"Make Up Your Own Holiday Day" on March 26 (or any day you choose). Try these novel ideas for celebrating:

- "Personal Indulgence Day" - get a manicure, facial, and massage. Eat your favorite comfort foods for dinner, including a rich, chocolate dessert.
- "Just Do It Day" - complete the chores or tasks you've been putting off.
- "New Me Day" - try a new activity, restaurant, and hairstyle.
- "PJ Day" - spend an entire day in your pajamas and slippers.

*E*scape to the movies alone. (If you go to a tear-jerker, you won't have to worry about anyone you know seeing you cry.)

♦

Take an unplanned "wellness day." On a whim, call in sick to work and make the day your own personal expression of fun, comfort and joy.

$\mathcal{S}$end signals to others that you want to be left alone.

- Retreat to the bathtub and hang a "Do Not Disturb" sign on the door.
- Have the courage to say, "This isn't a good time. Can we talk a little later?"
- Act like you're in a hurry to get somewhere.

*B*usy Woman's Break

Alexandra Stoddard, best-selling author of 18 books, including the classic *Living a Beautiful Life: 500 Ways to Add Elegance, Order, Beauty and Joy to Every Day of Your Life*, encourages daily rituals that harmonize our mind, body and soul. "When I am in need of rejuvenation, my favorite thing to do is to take a five-minute soak in the tub flavored with aromatic bath oils and herbs. It makes me feel invigorated for the rest of the day!"

Alexandra is a world-renowned interior designer and lifestyle philosopher. She is married and the proud mother of two grown daughters. Stoddard splits her time between homes in New York City and Stonington Village, CT.

***B*usy Woman's Break**

The supervisor of a Medicaid unit in New York's Westchester County Department of Social Services, Felicia Satchell took on an increased workload after several other offices closed.

"Keeping a journal has really helped me to reflect on the good times, as well as the stressful times. Trying to find time alone, even if it's just taking a walk, is also important to me," says the single mother of a teenage son. "I enjoy modern dancing because of its combination of creativity and physical exertion. It's something that challenges me outside of my regular work responsibilities. I also like to escape to a park or walk somewhere with trees or a lot of green. It helps me realize there's another world outside of what I'm involved in. I used to use my time unwisely, but I'm learning to divide my time so I'm accomplishing my priorities."

Felicia also volunteers at the Neuberger Museum of Art on the Purchase campus of State University of New York, where she serves on the Planning Committee of its annual fundraiser.

✦ *Your Private Treasures* ✦

PART 3

Attitude Adjusters
Getting a positive charge out of life

"Dwelling on the negative simply contributes to its power."

— *Shirley MacLaine*

Our attitudes are a reflection of ourselves—our moods, actions, choices, and the way other people see us. It's not bad to "have an attitude" as long as it's a positive one. By changing negative thoughts into opportunities, we can change our lives. These simple ideas can show you how to make the most out of the hand life has dealt you.

Start the day right by bringing in bagels
and gourmet coffee for the people in your
office or department.

◆

Ask to take part in interesting projects, and
try to delegate the ones that don't inspire you.

$\mathcal{M}$ake time for quick relaxation in the workplace.

+ Close your eyes and visualize yourself in a beautiful place—whether it's at the beach, in the mountains, or sailing on the water. Lose yourself as you see, hear, and feel the sights and sensations around you.
+ Do some stretches to ease tension in the back, neck, arms, and legs.
+ Take a few deep breaths before answering the telephone.
+ Give a co-worker a hand massage, and have her return the favor.

If you're unhappy in your job, recognize when it's time to move on. You do have a choice.

◆

Don't go to work when you're sick. You won't be at your best, and no one in your office wants to catch your cold.

$\mathcal{G}$row old gracefully. Follow the advice of baseball player Satchel Page, who said, "Age is a question of mind over matter. If you don't mind, it don't matter."

Smile sincerely and often. The simple act can make you feel happier.

✦

Play a good-spirited practical joke on a friend—but be prepared for a payback!

✦

Wear comfortable shoes.

$\mathcal{B}$egin each day with something that inspires or invigorates you, like listening to music, exercising, stretching, meditating, or reading over a hot cup of coffee.

Stop to pet a familiar, friendly dog in your neighborhood. Studies show that canine affection can actually lower your blood pressure.

◆

Make a scrapbook, collage, or bulletin board full of your favorite quotes and inspirations.

$\mathscr{G}$ive unto others—whether it's an intentional or random act of kindness. Doing good always helps you feel better about yourself. Here's a small list citing some of the endless possibilities:

- Get an organ donor card.
- Shovel your neighbor's sidewalk after a snowstorm.
- Give blood.
- Pay tolls for the next few cars that follow you.
- Be a "Secret Santa" at any time of year to cheer up a co-worker, friend, or family member when they're feeling blue.
- Make a casserole for the new mother down the street.

$\mathcal{R}$emember that you have a life outside the office. Decorate your office or cubicle with personal mementos and photos.

◆

Take a deep breath. For the most relaxing results, breathe through your diaphragm, expanding the belly, and exhale completely. Repeat several times.

$\mathcal{V}$isualize success. Close your eyes and imagine the positive outcome of a goal you're working toward—whether it's losing 50 pounds or completing a proposal for a lucrative, new job. This technique can make long-term goals easier to stick with and keep routine tasks from becoming chores. The key is believing that you can do it!

*U*nleash the child within.

- Read a Calvin & Hobbes anthology.
- Watch an episode of "The Brady Bunch."
- Make snow angels.
- Go to a playground. Slide down the slide and swing as high as you can on the swing set.
- Rent a classic Disney video.
- Buy a bell for your bike.
- Go to an amusement park and ride the merry-go-round.

$\mathcal{M}$ake chores less mundane. Turn on the stereo and clean to the beat. Or, challenge your partner to a contest to see who can set the land-speed record for emptying the trash (and be sure to agree on a reward for the winner).

◆

Keep a kaleidoscope handy to chase away the blues. It will help you see all the bright colors behind the clouds.

Thrill 'em with kindness, love, and respect. Most of the time, these gifts will come back to you in spades. When they don't, at least you know you took the high road.

◆

Lighten up! Don't sweat the small stuff. Is what you're worrying about right now really worth your time and energy? Or could you be concentrating on something much more fulfilling?

$\mathcal{D}$on't let the critics hold you back. When I first started doing seminars, I would agonize over a critical comment on my evaluations—even when it was one out of 100! Although I knew I couldn't please everyone, I still wanted to try. Then a friend helped me realize that if I made a person angry or confused, it means I touched them in some way. Now I know that my critics are often the people who need to hear my message the most. Maybe yours are, too. Focus on getting your message and feelings out there. You have something to offer. Let it be heard!

ℬusy Woman's Break

In a career that continually spans print, radio, TV, and film, media psychiatrist Carole Lieberman, M.D., is the nation's preeminent authority on the psychology of showbiz. When she's not seeing patients in her Beverly Hills office, you might find Carole hosting her own radio show, consulting on a television or movie script, appearing on a national talk show, or writing a book. An outspoken leader against violence in the media, she is also co-founder of H.O.P.E. (Hollywood Organizes for Positive Entertainment). Here's how this busy woman heals herself.

"Trapped on the little wheels of our cages, it's easy to lose sight of how important it is to get off—until we no longer can," she explains. "Horseback riding, skiing, rocky road ice cream, and sex (though not necessarily in this order) are my favorite ways to find renewal. By shaking the cobwebs loose, they help me find the way back to my soul and remember what's really important."

$\mathcal{B}$usy Woman's Break

"There's a fine line between being self-centered and centered. That's why I try to do things that bring out the best in myself," says Jill Smith, co-owner (with her husband) of **Buckeye Beans & Herbs**, a multi-million dollar company that makes whimsical pastas, beans and soup mixes. At her home in Spokane, WA, Jill is also a wife, mother of two, potter, author, soccer player, and Arabian horse breeder. Although she takes all of her roles seriously, she always makes time for fun. In fact, **Buckeye's** mission is "to make people smile"—and Jill leads by example.

"We believe that silly breaks are just as important as coffee breaks. That's why I often blow bubbles when I'm talking on the phone or wear a set of big plastic ears or Groucho glasses to meetings. We also sponsor 'Wacky Wednesdays' during our busy season. Each Wednesday something fun happens —whether we all wear plaid or treat our employees to free cookies," she says. "If you can't laugh at yourself, you shouldn't be in business. Through frivolous fun, we're able to stay creative, reduce stress, and treat our customers right. That's the art of doing good business."

✦ *Your Attitude Adjusters* ✦

PART 4

Image Enhancers
Looking and feeling your best

"Styles, like everything else, change. Style doesn't."
—*Linda Ellerbee*

It's what's on the inside that counts. But looking and feeling your best on the outside also reflects to others your true beauty. This chapter will help you discover your own personal style and ways to treat your body right. I guess getting "turned inside out" isn't so bad after all.

Take a few minutes to stretch every day. Relaxing your muscles also helps to refresh your mind.

✦

Participate in a fitness activity that benefits a worthy cause, like the March of Dimes Walk-A-Thon or Race for the Cure.

*W*ear a signature item that exudes your personal style. My "signatures" are one-of-a-kind pins that spark conversation and compliments wherever I go. (They also give friends and family a no-fail gift idea when the holidays roll around.)

◆

Wear only the clothes that make you look or feel your best. Give away all the others to your friends or a women's charity.

Satisfy weekday munchies and stave off extra pounds by packing a healthy snack stash for work. Your grab bag could include celery sticks filled with low-fat cream cheese, hard pretzels with gourmet mustard for dipping, fruit juice, hard candies, flavored rice cakes, air-popped popcorn, fat-free hot cocoa mix, or applesauce cups—to name a few.

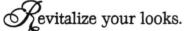 evitalize your looks.

- ✦ For a burst of natural-looking highlights, shampoo in a semi-permanent hair color one shade lighter than your natural tone.
- ✦ Buy one great suit and dress that make you look fabulous.
- ✦ Splurge on accessories like whimsical pins, bold scarves, and stylish shoes.
- ✦ Make your smile sparkle. Ask your dentist about safe, effective techniques for whitening your teeth.

*W*ear sexy lingerie under your most
casual clothes.

◆

Get seven to eight hours of sleep every night.

◆

Smooth on scented body lotion instead
of perfume.

Savor casual days at home. You (and your partner) will appreciate the sexy, stylish comfort of this irresistible lounge wear.

+ A man's oxford shirt and big, thick socks.
+ A plush terry cloth robe.
+ A satin and velour pajama set.
+ Sweatpants paired with a white tank top.

$\mathcal{T}$ry a temporary hair color to change your look risk-free.

✦

Try a bold, new hairdo. If you're unsure about the style, go to a salon that offers computerized programs to "test drive" several new dos.

$\mathcal{S}$plurge on a session or two with a personal trainer. She can help you set fitness goals and tone up those trouble spots.

✦

Treat yourself to a manicure or pedicure— even if you have to do it yourself.

Go makeup free for a day. We often forget how naturally beautiful we are.

◆

Save up for one expensive piece of jewelry that will brighten up everything from ball gowns to blue jeans.

$\mathcal{M}$ake a positive impression without saying a word.

- ✦ Practice proper posture.
- ✦ Smile, smile, smile.
- ✦ Shake hands firmly.
- ✦ Wear clothes that make you feel confident.

$\mathscr{E}$very once in a while, buy something on a delightful impulse. You can't be practical every single day!

◆

Always, always try on clothes before you buy them—or before you throw away that catalog return slip. If you don't love the way it looks on you, pass it up!

$\mathcal{T}$ry two sure ways to boost your image on an off-day: a bold lipstick and a pair of whimsical, dangling earrings.

◆

Give yourself a foot massage when you kick off your heels after a hard day's work. Use a scented gel or lotion to invigorate your "soles."

Busy Woman's Break

"There's no question about it. Working out with a fitness instructor has done more for my mental health than anything that I've done since I got into a high-stress occupation. It's absolutely marvelous," says Marilyn Moats Kennedy, managing partner of **Career Strategies,** a 20-year-old consulting firm based in Wilmette, IL. She's a woman who knows about the often grueling demands of the workplace. A wife and working mother, Marilyn is the author of six career development books and publisher of a monthly news-letter on career planning, job hunting, and office politics. She makes more than 150 presentations a year, writes a column for *Across the Board* magazine, and fre-quently contributes to many national publications.

"Exercise is a gift I give myself. I wouldn't even consider doing it alone. My trainer motivates me to get a much better workout, and I don't have to worry about little hassles, like keeping count."

ℬusy Woman's Break

Noel de Caprio, owner of **Noelle Spa for Beauty & Wellness** in Stamford, CT, is an expert in the art of pampering others—as well as herself. Pampering provides needed respite for a woman who supervises a staff of more than 130 employees, serves on numerous boards, develops beauty products, and helps other entrepreneurs successfully enter the day spa business.

"When I need an image boost, I put a sign on the bathroom door that says 'Gone Away.' Then I light an aromatherapy candle, put on soft music, dim the lights, and fill up the tub with warm water. I make sure that my bath pillow is blown up and that I have a large towel ready for when I come out," she explains. What follows is a soothing, half-hour ritual that includes a facial masque, foot scrub, relaxation exercise, foot massage, and back stretch. Confides Noel, "When I finally put the lights up, I look at the glow on my face and feel the relaxation emanate throughout my entire body."

✦ Your Image Enhancers ✦

PART 5

Powerful Inspirations
Opening yourself up to endless possibilities

"The future belongs to those who believe in the beauty of their dreams."

—Eleanor Roosevelt

Positive affirmations can unleash your creativity, open your mind, and lift your spirit. What's more, they're quick, easy, and effective forms of stress management. Pick one of the following affirmations to recite and reflect upon each day. I guarantee it will open a new window on your world.

Believe in yourself, for you have talents and gifts that can make a unique contribution to the world.

◆

Count your blessings. The quickest way to have a better life is to appreciate the life you already have.

The longest journey begins with one small step. Set small goals toward a bigger goal and go for it!

◆

Believe in miracles. Once you open your heart to the possibility, you'll find that they happen every day.

$\mathcal{L}$ook at problems in a different light. You have three choices to make:

- Do nothing and continue to complain and be miserable.
- Do nothing, but make the conscious choice to let go and make the best of things.
- Act to change the situation.

Even subconsciously, you're always making one of these choices. By recognizing that you are in control, you can choose more wisely.

Slow down for a moment each day. Relish the amazing sights and sounds around you. The world is full of magic if you just take the time to observe it.

◆

Right now, give yourself a pat on the back for something you accomplished today.

*D*ream big!

◆

Accept that you can never be perfect,
but strive to be your best.

◆

Relish the moment. It will slip away all
too quickly.

Stop saying "coulda, woulda, shoulda."
It only means you didn't. Next time, take
action or let it go gracefully.

✦

Accept a compliment graciously and sincerely.
You devalue this kind gesture if you brush
it aside.

When others can't give you the support you need, it's a gift you must give to yourself.

◆

Don't hesitate to ask others for help or advice. Most people are flattered and honored to give it.

$\mathcal{E}$nd every day by answering these questions.

- ✦ What did I contribute today?
- ✦ What am I grateful for?
- ✦ What am I looking forward to tomorrow?

$\mathcal{A}$ct like the person you want to be.

◆

Value every person's life as you value your own.

◆

Only make promises you can surely keep.

*U*nderstand that stress is your response to daily demands. That's actually good news, because it means that you're in control. Nothing can make you feel bad unless you let it.

What gift can you give yourself today that you've never allowed yourself before—the permission to cry, the ability to say "no," the realization you're someone special? Whatever it is, you're worth it!

◆

Create your own definition of success.
If you're doing what you love, be proud of it.
If you're not, ask why.

$\mathcal{S}$top making excuses. They'll stop you in your tracks and take your dreams away with them.

✦

Dance with life as your partner. Although some days you may feel like you have two left feet, you can still keep in step.

ℬusy Woman's Break

When I asked Consuelo Mack, anchor and editor of the nationally syndicated television program, "The Wall Street Journal Report," how she finds time to relax, she replied, "At first, I thought, 'Do I relax and rejuvenate anymore?' It's getting harder and harder. Then I paused and realized I am still doing things that keep me on as even a keel as I can be."

She explains, "If you don't step off the fast track, you lose control. As it becomes harder and harder to stop, it becomes more necessary to do so. I go to church to reflect and correct, exercise for strength and release, and relax with family for love and sustenance."

Consuelo, an award-winning business reporter, is also the host of the PBS documentary series, "Emerging Powers."

$\mathscr{B}$usy Woman's Break

"Everyone gets one chance in life. Be the best you can be. Work hard for what you want. Live your passion, and everything wonderful in life will follow." Marianne Szymanski believes in and lives by that credo. As founder and president of **Toy Tips, Inc.** in Milwaukee, WI, Marianne is an international toy expert whose firm conducts ongoing research on toy popularity, safety, and trends in the United States and Europe. She is a contributor on "Good Morning America," FOX-TV, and America On-Line and frequently guest lectures at universities nationwide.

In 1996, Marianne received the Small Business Administration's *Young Entrepreneur of the Year Award.* She is currently at work on her first book. For other busy women, Marianne offers this empowering affirmation: "Success is not something that is given to you. You must make it happen."

✦ *Your Powerful Inspirations* ✦

PART 6

Passionate Kisses
Keeping your love alive

"I truly feel that there are as many ways of loving as there are people in the world and as there are days in the lives of those people."

—*Mary S. Calderone*

For better or worse, in sickness and in health, for richer or poorer…keeping those promises alive is what love is all about. If you sometimes feel like your romantic well has gone dry, this chapter showers you with suggestions for giving special Valentines all year long.

Show some unexpected respect. Surprise your mate with something totally out of character. Try biting your tongue the next time you find clothes lying on the floor, watch an entire "Monday Night Football" game, or let him get lost without asking him to stop for directions.

$\mathcal{K}$eep love alive. Make a scrapbook of love letters, cards, photos, notes, and postcards that chronicles your romance from its inception.

◆

Rekindle musical memories. Host a "music hour" for two, in which you and your partner alternate playing your favorite blasts from the past.

Say "I love you" without saying a word.

- Spoon in bed.
- Look longingly into his eyes.
- Give him a bear hug.
- Listen, really listen, to what your partner has to say.

Absence makes the heart grow fonder. Give each other some space by spending a few days apart.

◆

Agree to a "mutual kindness day" during which you can only say positive things to each other. Any slip-up requires compensation of some sort, like getting squirted with a water gun, paying a dollar, or doing a chore.

Turn on the stereo and dance cheek-to-cheek in your own living room.

✦

Wake up early to watch the sun rise or talk over coffee.

✦

Sit in the back row of a movie theater and make out.

$\mathcal{S}$pend a lazy day with your sweetie.

- Sleep late.
- Enjoy coffee and croissants in bed.
- Read the Sunday paper together.
- Give each other a massage.
- Watch football and order pizza.
- Shower together.
- Pop popcorn and rent a classic video.

Give a gift that evokes a special memory. Each year on your wedding anniversary, wrap an object that symbolizes an important event during the past year—like the keys to the new house you bought, a baby bootie in honor of your pregnancy, or a seashell from the beach where you took a romantic vacation.

$\mathscr{G}$et "in the mood" with music. Try these sultry suggestions:

- ✦ "Unchained Melody" by the Righteous Brothers
- ✦ "I Go Crazy" by Paul Davis
- ✦ Ravel's "Bolero"
- ✦ Theme from "Cat People" by David Bowie
- ✦ Anything by Sting or Seal

Say three, simple, three-word phrases that mean the world:

- ✦ I love you.
- ✦ I was wrong.
- ✦ I'm so sorry.

$\mathcal{L}$et him know he's on your mind even when you're apart. Stuff little notes into his suitcase before he leaves on a business trip. Or if you're going away, leave notes around the house in places you know he'll find them.

$\mathcal{D}$eclare your sweetheart "King for the Day" and do exactly what he wants for an entire Saturday.

◆

Play games—from Trivial Pursuit to Twister—to sharpen your wits and spark a little friendly competition.

*W*ear his clothes on lazy, lounging days.

◆

Learn how to give him a clean, close,
nick-free shave.

◆

Ask him to paint your toenails pink.

Surprise him in the morning with a hot breakfast before work or in the evening with a cozy, candlelight dinner for two.

✦

Engage in important discussions in the bathroom or while lying in bed. The location itself can ease the tension and help you stay focused.

Prevent holiday hassles.
- Alternate whose family you will visit on major holidays. It's just too hard to do it all.
- Have both families over to your place.
- Escape from everyone to spend a romantic holiday on your own.

ℬusy Woman's Break

Julia Haller, M.D., wears many hats. In addition to her full-time career as a retinal surgeon at Johns Hopkins' Wilmer Eye Institute, she is a wife, mother of five, Sunday school teacher, and volunteer hospice physician. She serves on the Board of Trustees of Maryland's Bryn Mawr School and is on the Board of the Baltimore City Medical Society Foundation. Haller is also a member of several national medical societies, and is helping to plan the 20th reunion for her undergraduate class at Princeton University.

So how in the world do she and her husband (who is also an ophthalmologist) sustain their level of intimacy and romance? "There are three primary things that we do," Julia explains. "First and foremost, we try to set aside one night a week for just the two of us. To keep things creative, we alternate planning the date—which can range from dinner and a movie to ballroom dancing lessons. My husband and I have also discovered that playing doubles tennis is a great way to spend time together, get some exercise, and socialize with our friends. In addition, since we're both in the same field, we try to attend professional meetings together. When we're in exotic or romantic locales, we tack a few extra days on to the trip to explore the area together."

$\mathcal{B}$usy Woman's Break

To say that Laura Luckert has her hands full is an understatement. As mother of a five-year-old daughter and newborn quadruplet sons, she works a nearly 24-hour day sprinkled with much-needed sleep breaks. Although weekday help from friends and family lightens the load, "couple time" for Laura and her husband, who owns a trucking business in Baltimore, MD, comes at a premium.

"It was hard in the beginning to keep our relationship working," she explains. "Now that the babies are in high chairs, I can feed them all before my husband comes home from work. That way, we can share a more peaceful dinner together with our daughter. When the weather is nice, we take walks and talk while pushing the boys in their strollers. Every few months, when my sister comes to help out, we try to escape from it all. We've spent a long weekend in the Bahamas and, just recently, took an overnight trip to Atlantic City. At home, when the kids are napping, we try to steal a few private moments in the shower or the garage. Since we have so little time alone, we try to savor every moment."

✦ *Your Passionate Kisses* ✦

PART 7

Great Strides
Expanding your mind

"Study as if you were going to live forever. Live as if you were going to die tomorrow."

—*Maria Mitchell*

There are few things as gratifying as learning a new art or mastering an existing skill. Taking this step on the path to greater fulfillment opens a world of possibilities. Start your powerful future today. These suggestions will show you how.

Go to a museum seeking to learn something. When you return home, write a journal entry about what most inspired you or piqued your interest.

◆

Ideas strike at all hours. Put a pencil and paper on your nightstand, keep a pocket tape recorder in your car, and stash a pen and notepad in your purse. (I even keep a pen and notepad in the bathroom!)

$\mathcal{L}$earn something new. Many community colleges or public school systems offer adult non-credit courses at reasonable rates.

◆

Watch a how-to program to learn a new skill. The Learning Channel and PBS offer shows on home improvement, cooking, decorating, sewing, painting, and much more.

Take a risk—wear that tiny string bikini, ask for a raise, go parasailing, or take the first step to starting your own business. As Eleanor Roosevelt said, "You must do the thing you think you cannot do."

Take a learning vacation. A number of hotels offer cooking instruction packages, wine and beer tastings, and historical tours.

◆

Take on new responsibilities at work. Ask to be involved in an interesting project or offer to serve on a committee.

$\mathcal{S}$urf the net. You can gather useful information on any subject—from starting a home-based business and picking winning stocks to booking a vacation and choosing the right pet. You can get started by checking out these sites, which can pool personalized news and information from a variety of sources.

Pathfinder (http://www.pathfinder.com)
Pointcast (http://www.pointcast.com)
NewsPage (http://pnp.individual.com)

$\mathcal{B}$uy a dictionary and learn a new word
every day.

◆

Take advantage of free lectures and
cultural events.

◆

Keep current. Subscribe to a newspaper
or news magazine.

$\mathcal{S}$et aside fifteen minutes each day to complete a task that yields positive improvements.

- ✦ Learn to program your VCR.
- ✦ Do 20 push-ups.
- ✦ Pick out a new recipe to make this weekend.
- ✦ Pray or meditate.

$\mathscr{T}$hinking of pursuing a new hobby or line of work? Subscribe to a related magazine, newspaper, or newsletter to learn more about it.

✦

Go for a degree—whether it's a G.E.D. or a Ph.D. It could be the key that opens the door to your dream.

Expand your network and enhance your skills by joining a professional society or common interest group.

◆

Explore the history and traditions of other cultures. Attend an ethnic festival, dine on regional cuisine, or attend a cultural exhibition.

Make your self-talk more empowering by turning negative thoughts into motivation for personal growth and improvement.

+ Change "I'm too fat," to "I want to look great in my bathing suit this year."
+ Change "I'm so stressed out," to "I need to do something special for myself today."
+ Change "Why do terrible things always happen to me," to "I'm a much stronger person now."
+ Change "I can't do everything that's expected of me," to "I need to concentrate on my most fulfilling priorities."

When you travel, build up your roster of personal and professional contacts. They could turn into friends, valuable resources, or business partners.

◆

Listen carefully to what others have to say. By doing so, you'll open your mind to a realm of new possibilities and experiences.

Update your resume at least once a year.

✦

Learn how to change a flat tire.

✦

Recognize the secret for getting what
you want—ask for it!

Busy Woman's Break

Tired of living with the daily demands of being a television news reporter and anchorwoman, Marissa Leinart decided to take a leap. She accepted the post of media relations director for **Food for the Hungry,** an Arizona-based relief and development organization that helps the poorest people in more than 25 third world countries. "I made the change because of stress," she confides. "There is a season for everything. Sometimes people reach a point where they need to do something different. There are trade offs, but I chose to take them because the benefits far outweigh the seemingly glamorous perks of my old job. Since I left TV, I've never been happier. I now have less stress and more time to enjoy life with my family."

After the birth of her first child, Marissa decided to take another leap and become a stay-at-home mom. She remains busy running a home-based video production company. Through it all, Marissa manages to keep her head above water and her priorities in line. "There's no other country where dreams are so obtainable," she says. "I attend to my personal growth and rejuvenation by reading the *Bible,* praying, and being thankful for all of the wonderful things I have."

ℬusy Woman's Break

"In spite of perceived limitations, within each of us lies an unlimited reservoir of creativity, intelligence, and energy," says Veronica Butler, M.D., a divorced mother of one and Medical Director of the Family Practice Center in Ottumwa, IA. Veronica is also co-author of the book, *A Woman's Best Medicine,* and serves in several other medical roles in her area.

Her prescription for healing the wounds of busy women? "As a physician I know that Transcendental Meditation offers the only scientifically proven method to tap into nature's perfection, stillness, and bliss. The fulfillment of our dreams is our birthright."

✦ *Your Great Strides* ✦

PART 8

Everyday Riches
Savoring life's little treasures

"It isn't the great big pleasures that count the most; it's making a great deal out of the little ones."

—*Jean Webster*

When was the last time you stared into the starry sky on a moonlit night? Gazed across the room into your spouse's eyes like you did when you first met? Relished in completing your household chores? Many times, these simple treasures get buried in life's everyday activities. This chapter offers direction to help you uncover the joy in the simplest accomplishments and rediscover the beauty in the world we so often take for granted.

Wake up an hour early once a week to have some quiet time to read, relax, exercise, or do chores.

◆

Follow the lead of your favorite feline. Lie on the floor in a beam of sunlight or steal a few moments for a cat nap.

$\mathcal{S}$leep naked.

✦

Watch the sunrise.

✦

Fall asleep in a hammock.

Make good use of a rainy weekend.

+ Read a great thriller from start to finish.
+ Rent the videos of the movies you never had a chance to see in the theater.
+ Try styling your hair in a different way.
+ Balance your checkbook down to the penny.
+ Prepare some make-ahead meals for the coming week.
+ Read *The New York Times* Sunday edition.

Walk barefoot on the beach or in cool,
spring grass.

♦

Press a leaf or flower in a book where it will
delight you later.

♦

Keep a bouquet of fresh flowers in your
home or office.

Take a real day off. Do absolutely nothing but lounge and loaf. No chores, work, errands, or alarm clocks allowed!

◆

On a cool night, bundle up in warm, fluffy blankets and sleep with the windows open.

$\mathscr{B}$e news free. Go an entire day without turning on the television, radio, or picking up a newspaper.

◆

Change into your jammies and slippers the moment you get home from work.

On a clear summer night, lie on your back
and gaze at the stars.

◆

Snuggle up on the couch with your dog or cat.

◆

Read by the flickering flames of a fire.

$\mathcal{S}$avor the pleasures of being an adult. Do a thing or two that would make your parents shudder.

- Jump in the swimming pool right after eating.
- Stay up past your bedtime.
- Spoil your appetite.
- Leave food on your plate.
- Buy sugary breakfast cereals just to get the prize inside.

131

$\mathcal{F}$or classy correspondence, get personalized stationery printed.

◆

Look for the rainbow after a summer shower.

◆

Gather neighborhood singers for a yuletide caroling session.

$\mathcal{F}$or warmth from the inside out, buy the softest, most whimsical blanket you can find—and invite your sweetie inside for cuddling.

◆

Record a creative message on your answering machine by incorporating your favorite music, sound effects, or your children's voices.

$\mathcal{E}$at on the patio, weather permitting.

◆

Take a long lunch.

◆

Sing in the shower.

$\mathcal{M}$ake the most of your photographic skills.

+ Blow up your favorite prints, buy matching frames, and create a personalized wall or tabletop display.
+ Spruce up photo albums with clippings, mementoes, and colorful headings and captions.
+ Dare to be different. Buy a roll of black and white film for your next family photo shoot.

*B*usy Woman's Break

Rebecca Maddox's career path from corporate senior executive, to intrapreneur creating a business within a business, to entrepreneur and business owner, has established her as a highly visible role model for women across America. She is author of the book, *Inc. Your Dreams,* and is the president and co-founder of **Capital Rose Inc.**, a company that provides women business owners access to financing, information, and related products, and works with Fortune 500 clients to capitalize on the growing opportunities in the women's market.

"I used to think the rest of the world was responsible for my 'unbalanced' existence. Once I became a business owner, I quickly realized only I could bring the balance I so often dreamed about to my life," she says. "I now realize that balance is about actively choosing how I spend each and every moment of my life. It is no longer something that happens to me, but something I do for myself with great joy. I have learned that you succeed in your chosen career by experiencing everything you can from life. When I am starting to feel stale or bored, which is always a signal that I need a time-out, I go off in the middle of the afternoon and do something physical. In the spring and summer, I enjoy weed-whacking on my farm in Chester Springs, PA. I find it relaxing, it clears my mind, my thinking is uninterrupted and I get the added benefit of accomplishing something while I rejuvenate."

Busy Woman's Break

Judsen Culbreth knows what's it's like to be a working mother—so much so that she shares her expertise with other moms as editor-in-chief of *Working Mother* magazine and as work/family contributing editor on NBC's "Today" show. "I believe that the best gift a mother can give her child is happiness," she explains. "In order to do that she has to be happy herself."

Judsen has testified on behalf of working mothers in the Washington, D.C., Congressional hearing on retirement income, was a spokesperson for the Family and Medical Leave Act, and has spoken at conventions across the country. She serves on the March of Dimes Media Advisory Board and the Board of the Child Care Action Campaign. She is a member of the International Women's Forum, the Women's Media Group, and the American Society of Magazine Editors.

Amidst her myriad responsibilities, Judsen still finds time to enjoy life's simple pleasures. She says, "Now that my children are ten and sixteen, I have more time to indulge myself. I do strength training twice a week (sometimes with my daughter); I teach Sunday School; I go to Bible study classes once a week; I belong to a book club; and my hobby is genealogy. I find it relaxing to do the things I love."

Your Everyday Riches

PART 9

Lasting Impressions
Embarking on a journey of self-discovery

"You can live a lifetime and, at the end of it, know more about other people than you know about yourself."
—*Beryl Markham*

In my quest to rediscover life's magic moments, the most meaningful step was delving inside to recognize my gifts, needs, and deepest desires. The affirming power of introspection can help you, too, build a sense of confidence and motivation that will propel you toward your dreams. Through the following lessons, you'll learn to listen to the whispers from within—and turn them into shouts of delight.

Make a weekly journal entry entitled, "The Week in Review" to record your feelings, triumphs, and stumbling blocks during the past week. Conclude by writing a few things you'd like to focus on—emotionally or physically—to make the coming week more fulfilling. At the end of the year, instead of making New Year's resolutions that fade, compile a retrospective of the things you're most proud of (large and small) in the year gone by. At the end, write a paragraph or two describing what you'd like to do to make the new year incredible!

$\mathcal{S}$et goals and define your aspirations in each area of your life—personal, family, professional, financial, health, and spiritual.

◆

Make a list of your strengths. You've been blessed with many, many talents. Write down at least 15, hopefully more.

$\mathcal{O}$rganize a meeting of the minds. If you're going through an important or difficult transition—like a career change, divorce, or move—gather an informal "board of directors" to help you chart your course.

+ Invite people you trust and admire— from friends and family to business associates and colleagues.
+ Treat the group to a special breakfast, lunch, or dinner, then spend a few hours going over your ideas, brainstorming, or developing an action plan. If the meeting will take longer, splurge by offering a weekend getaway, or rent a charming facility for the day.
+ Have a clear idea of what you want to accomplish during the session so you stay on track.
+ Show the participants how much you appreciate their "free advice" by sending thank-you notes or special gifts a few days later—and be sure to keep all of them posted on your progress.

*C*ure your "yes" reflex. Here's how:
- ✦ The next time someone asks you to add another responsibility to your overloaded plate, don't answer right away. Tell the person you'll get back to them in a few minutes, hours, or days.
- ✦ Take time to evaluate the situation and determine whether it will add or take away from your priorities. Then and only then, give the person an answer you can live with.
- ✦ Go for the win-win scenario. If you really want the job, maybe you could extend the deadline or work on it with a colleague to ease the load. If you honestly don't have the time, refer the person to a capable associate.
- ✦ Remember that many people would prefer that you say "no" rather than giving the project only a half-hearted effort.

$\mathcal{C}$hallenge yourself. Ask your friends, family, clients, and colleagues for constructive feedback. You won't know where to improve unless you know what's going wrong. And, their words may help you remember to give yourself credit for work well done.

◆

Reflect on the "moments of truth" in your life. What changes and revelations did they spark in you?

*I*magine passing away at a ripe old age. It may feel morbid, but answering these questions can provide profound direction for your future.

+ What would you have wanted to accomplish in your lifetime?
+ What would you want people to remember you for?
+ What would you want your epitaph to read?
+ How can you live your life right now to make these things a reality—whether you die tomorrow or in fifty years?

Make a three-ring "dream binder." Fill it with magazine clippings of ideas for your dream home, must-see travel destinations, new haircuts to try, the prettiest flowers for your spring garden, or success stories that inspire you.

Keep a diary by your bed to record the
messages in your dreams.

✦

Make a list of people who have inspired you
and why.

✦

Create your life's motto. If you could print
your personal slogan on a bumper sticker,
what would it say?

147

$\mathscr{M}$editate for 15 minutes each day. You don't have to light incense or sit in an uncomfortable position on a cold, hard floor. Meditation is an activity that involves deep concentration in the present moment. Here are some ideas to get you started:

+ Write in your journal.
+ Sit or lie in front of a window and relish in the beauty of nature—or go to a park and sit in its most scenic spot.
+ Savor every bite of a delicious dessert.
+ Sit on a pillow, put on soft music, and close your eyes.

The key to meditation is to breathe slowly and banish thoughts from your mind. When you emerge from your relaxed state, you'll feel a sense of centeredness.

$\mathcal{I}$n your journal, list your values—then challenge yourself to live by them.

◆

Write a creative essay about your favorite color. Why do you like it so much? How does it reflect your personality?

149

*E*scape on a personal retreat. It's your opportunity to design a trip that is all your own—with no interruptions and no one else to please. For the best results, follow these tips:

+ Make the trip at least a weekend long.
+ Take time to see the sights, take a nap, eat comfort foods, or dine out at a nearby restaurant.
+ Include some introspective exercises.
+ Choose the right destination—somewhere that inspires you with its beauty, solitude, or bustle.
+ Make it an annual event. I can tell you from personal experience, it's a vacation you'll look forward to year after year.

$\mathcal{W}$rite a personal mission statement that
will help you live your life purposefully.
Read your statement as an affirmation
every morning.

◆

Think of a time when you mustered up your
personal courage. Recall the skills you used to
give you confidence when other problems
come your way.

151

Re-evaluate your definition of success. Does it mean a luxury car and a big house filled with lots of children? Or does it mean personal satisfaction with your career, having time left over to for a social life, or being able to take one nice vacation a year? No definition is wrong. The key is to be clear about what it will take to get what you want, as well as the consequences when you do. This vision provides direction on the road to success—and prevents unwanted detours.

Have a heart-to-heart talk with your parents to uncover clues, habits, and activities from your childhood. They may help you recognize familiar patterns or rekindle a forgotten pleasure.

Busy Woman's Break

Professional coach Laura Berman Fortgang advises her executive and entrepreneurial clients to practice ten daily habits of well-being. The exercise involves making a list of ten things that, if you did them, would make your life more organized and enjoyable. Laura explains, "The list should include those things that always fall through the cracks in the name of not having enough time—even though they're still important and rewarding. The simple act of writing them down makes them easier to accomplish."

Laura's own daily list includes drinking eight glasses of water, connecting with a friend, putting things away, and moving her body in a fun, healthy way. When she's not running her business, **InterCoach Business Development & Training,** you might find Laura writing a soon-to-be-published business book, teaching classes through Coach University, serving as president of a local networking organization, performing in community theater, or stealing a few private moments with her husband in their Verona, NJ, home.

$\mathcal{B}$usy Woman's Break

As President of **Communication Strategies,** a 15-year-old PR/marketing firm in Roslyn Harbor, NY, Judith Machanik works from deadline to deadline. "That's why it's essential to have some techniques and tools to boost my spirit, refresh my soul, and give me peace of mind," she says. "I make an appointment with myself, put it on the calendar, and set aside that time for walking, reading, listening to music, meditating, or exercise. I am the most important 'client' I have, and I can't be there for others if I don't take care of myself."

Judith's many other roles include that of lecturer, seminar planner, wife, mother, and grandmother. In honor of her mother who died from breast cancer at age 39, Judith also volunteers her time to educate other women about prevention of the disease.

To maintain her positive attitude and self confidence, Judith keeps a "victory log" on her desk to record each victory—big and small: a lucrative contract, a strengthened relationship, a new idea, successful closure on a project, or an inspiring quote. She confides, "Personal renewal needs to be consistent and creative—and it does help."

✦ *Your Lasting Impressions* ✦

PART 10

Friendly Advice
Boosting companionship and comraderie

"Each friend represents a world in us, a world possibly not born before they arrive, and it is only by this meeting that a new world is born."

—*Anaïs Nin*

Our best friends share common interests, listen with a sympathetic ear, complement our strengths, and offer support and encouragement in our finest moments and greatest defeats. Whether you talk to a friend once a year or once a day, you know she'll always be there. A friend is a blessing who touches your very heart and soul. Following are ways to return this most precious gift.

*C*all an old friend from high school
or college.

◆

Gather around the piano or guitar for
a sing-a-long.

◆

Offer to babysit a friend's child for the
afternoon or evening.

Give the gift of reading. Books make great, personalized gifts. Surprise a friend with a special book you know she'll enjoy, but might not buy for herself.

◆

Send a special friend a small gift for no occasion. Everyone loves to receive surprises.

$\mathcal{P}$arty hardy! Everybody likes to get together with good friends, but who has the time to prepare? Here are some easy, inexpensive party ideas guaranteed to inspire comraderie:

- **Drive-in Party.** Lug the TV into the backyard, pop a couple of videos into the VCR, and serve popcorn, sodas, and Twizzlers. Ask friends to bring their own blankets and lawn chairs to watch the show.
- **Recipe Party.** You make the main entree and friends bring one of the other courses, such as an appetizer, salad, or dessert. Everybody brings enough copies of the recipe for their dish to go around.
- **Salad Bar Party.** Ask friends to bring one or two ingredients to create a spectacular salad. Serve with warm sourdough bread, a variety of dressings, and a sumptuous dessert.
- **Cookie Party.** Invite friends over to make dozens of delicious cookies. Split the proceeds among yourselves or donate them to a soup kitchen during the holidays.
- **Make Your Own Pizza Party.** You provide individual-size pizza crusts and cheese, and guests bring a variety of toppings. Serve with salad and some great micro-brewed beer.
- **Muffins in the Morning Party.** Bake a dozen muffins, brew a pot of coffee, and invite a few friends over for a morning cafe klatch. Follow up with a group walk, bike ride, or movie matinee.

$\mathcal{I}$f you're in a friendship that no longer supports you, it may be time to let it go gracefully. Don't be afraid. It could allow more time for a new, more meaningful relationship.

◆

Each week, for no reason at all, send at least one person a wonderful card—one that makes them laugh, reflect, or feel good about themselves.

$\mathcal{S}$park discussion with friends by pondering some intriguing questions:

- What would you do if you won the lottery?
- If you could meet God, what would you ask her or him?
- If you could be President, what is the first thing you would do?
- If you could have lunch with anyone, who would it be?
- If you were sure to achieve one thing in life, what would it be?

$\mathcal{G}$ive your best friend a back rub.

✦

Share your dreams and encourage each
other to soar.

✦

When your best friend asks your opinion,
be honest.

*I*nvite the girls over for a classic "chick flick night" with:

- *Fried Green Tomatoes* starring Jessica Tandy and Kathy Bates.
- *Thelma & Louise* starring Susan Sarandon and Geena Davis.
- *Waiting to Exhale* starring Angela Bassett and Whitney Houston.
- *Sense and Sensibility* starring Emma Thompson and Kate Winslet.
- *The Bridges of Madison County* starring Meryl Streep and Clint Eastwood.
- *The Mirror Has Two Faces* starring Barbra Streisand and Jeff Bridges.

Avoid negative friends or constant complainers. As much as you'd like to lift their spirits, they're more likely to bring you down.

◆

Form an informal "support group" of friends that meets once a month to discuss each other's trials and triumphs.

Take an adventure trip with your best friend. It's a sure way to strengthen your bond and learn wonderful, new things about each other.

◆

Go camping and take turns telling ghost stories by the light of an eerie, flickering fire.

The next time your best buddy comes down with a cold, try these creative ways to lift her spirits:

- ✦ Take over a cup of cheer—a ceramic mug filled with an assortment of herbal teas, honey-coated spoons, and a mini-pack of tissues.
- ✦ Give her some homemade chicken soup to warm her belly and a book of short stories to warm her heart.
- ✦ Offer to run some errands for her after you leave work.

*P*lay sports together. It's a great way to keep in touch and stay in shape.

◆

Create a mini-cookbook that includes your ten favorite recipes. Have it printed or copied on colored paper, and give one to each of your closest friends.

*H*elp a friend cure the blues or get out of a rut.

- ✦ Plan a Saturday trip to the shopping malls, a nearby hiking trail, or the beach.
- ✦ Put a card and a long-stemmed, yellow rose on her desk or doorstep.
- ✦ Give her an inspirational quote that you've had written in calligraphy and framed.

*B*usy Woman's Break

An internationally known author, career strategist, and change management consultant, Adele Scheele, Ph.D., encourages women to form "strategy groups" that foster support and encouragement on career and personal issues. She leads by example. "I rely a great deal on friends. As women, the more we do and the more we achieve, the more we need each other to share triumphs, despair, dilemmas, ideas, and just the general buoying up for the risk-taking that's involved in life."

Adele is director of the Career Center at California State University-Northridge. She is the author of *Skills for Success* and *Career Strategies for the Working Woman* and also serves on the boards of several women's organizations.

*B*usy Woman's Break

Cathey Graham, marketing director for Columbia Highland Hospital in Shreveport, LA, enjoys hopping on her Nordic Track early in the morning with her headphones tuned into her favorite tape. "It's the number-one form of relaxation I can find," says the single mother of a six-year-old boy. "The house is quiet, and the world feels like it hasn't quite woken up yet."

Cathey also enjoys sharing relaxation time with friends. "When we can find babysitters, we all hit our favorite Italian restaurant that has an outdoor deck. Even in the wintertime, the nice Southern weather here in Louisiana allows us to sit outside, sip a little Chianti, and chat about what we've all been up to."

In her "spare time," Cathey attends graduate school (where she is working toward a Master of Liberal Arts degree), volunteers as publicity chairman for various community projects,and is a freelance writer for several local publications.

✦ Your Friendly Advice ✦

PART 11

Time Savors
Making the most of each day

"I must govern the clock, not be governed by it."
—*Golda Meir*

No matter how hard we wish, we'll never find a way to slow the hands of time. We can, however, find ways to use time wisely. Although the ideas in this chapter are not magical in and of themselves, they may afford you more time for those that are.

*B*eat the crowds and shop in the privacy of your own home. Browse through the best of the catalogs you get in the mail and buy a special item for yourself or the perfect gift for a loved one. These catalogs are guaranteed to give you lots of wonderful options:

- *Smith & Hawken,* a gardener's dream catalog, 800-776-3336.
- *Seasons,* timeless gifts for everyone in the family (with a special emphasis on gifts for women), 800-776-9677.
- *The Territory Ahead,* stylish casual clothes for men and women, displayed amidst lush tropical scenery, 800-882-4323.
- *Signals,* gifts for fans of public television, 800-669-9696.

Go through your mail every day.
Immediately toss what you don't want
and act on or file the others.

✦

Make a list of everything you feel guilty
about. Analyze each item to see if it's worth
your time and energy. Give yourself
permission to drop the ones that aren't.

Don't get caught in the cleaning trap. It doesn't take blood, sweat, and tears to make your house appear neat as a pin. If you don't have a lot of time, small things can make a big difference—like making the bed, throwing away junk mail, wiping off the bathroom mirror, sweeping up dust bunnies, putting dirty dishes in the dishwasher, and throwing dirty clothes in the laundry basket instead of on the floor.

Give yourself a break. At least once or twice a year, hire someone to clean your house, wash your car, or mow the lawn.

◆

Every weekend, make a list of all the things you wish you had time for in the coming week—and schedule in at least one of them.

Be realistic about the things you can accomplish in one day. As much as we hate to admit it, we only have 24 hours.

✦

Get your priorities straight. Pare down your address book and calendar to include only those people and appointments most important to you.

$\mathcal{L}$earn to say "no" gracefully.

◆

File your income tax return early this year.

◆

Try your darndest to leave work on time.

Restructure your work day for peak performance.

+ Work on your toughest assignments during the hours when you feel the most productive and attentive.
+ Ask your boss about flex-time or telecommuting.
+ Exercise at least three times a week for more energy every day.

Take advantage of "down time" at work and home. When you're printing out long documents, booting up your computer, or waiting for water to boil, take those few minutes to open mail, return a phone call, or do some stretching. You'll find that these minutes multiply and may free up a half-hour to do something you really enjoy, like taking a walk or luxuriating in a hot bath.

*I*f you live your life by the calendar, schedule time for things that are non-work related, such as romantic dates, exercise, a manicure, lunches with friends, or activities with your children.

◆

Free yourself from the clock by taking off your watch the minute you get home from work.

$\mathscr{C}$ombine activities to achieve more of your goals.

- ✦ If you want to exercise and spend quality time with your children, plan a family hike in a nearby park.
- ✦ If you need to go grocery shopping and want to catch up on the latest bestseller, pop the book-on-tape into your portable tape player and listen to it as you roam the aisles.
- ✦ If you want more private time and need to buy a new dress, soak in the bathtub while leafing through your favorite clothing catalogs.
- ✦ If you need to cook dinner and want to keep in touch with family members, call your sister while the casserole bakes in the oven.

*N*o time for a bath? Make your shower your sanctuary by using a scented body wash, a back scrub brush, and a variable shower head that gives you options for soothing pressure and pleasure. Dry off with the fluffiest towels you can find.

◆

Pare down your social calendar. If you really need some private time, tell the hostess of the party you already have plans—even if those plans are to stay at home and watch an old movie. If you do attend the party, try leaving a little early or arriving fashionably late.

$\mathscr{T}$ake control of your work day.

- ✦ If you're trying to complete an important project uninterrupted, put a "Do Not
  Disturb" sign outside your door, and let
  your voice mail pick up your phone calls.
- ✦ If you need to make or return a call, but
  don't actually have to talk to the person,
  call when you know their voice mail or
  answering machine will pick up. It's a
  productive way of making use of technology and time. In most cases, the
  other person will probably appreciate
  the gesture, too.
- ✦ To catch up and really concentrate on
  projects, keep at least one day a week
  meeting-free.

*I*nvite three friends over for a "make-ahead meal" party. Each person brings enough ingredients to prepare one of her favorite casseroles times four. In the end, everyone leaves with four delicious dishes to freeze and serve in the coming weeks.

$\mathscr{D}$o one chore each weekday evening.
The extra effort allows you to reserve one day
over the weekend for pure relaxation and
rejuvenation.

✦

Carry a book of short stories, poetry, or affirmations. It will come in handy if you have to
stand in long lines, wait for appointments, or
commute to and from work.

ℬusy Woman's Break

For more than 12 years, Vicki Sorenson directed the **National Institute of Fitness**, a St. George, UT health spa, which she and her husband founded and owned until 1994. Vicki is now a certified protocol expert who offers counseling and expertise to Utah organizations with international ties. The mother of four stepchildren, she is the author of two books and serves on the National Advisory Council for Weber State University and on the board for the Utah Contemporary Dance Theatre.

This busy woman doesn't have a defined regimen for relaxation and renewal—but she does abide by one rule. "I find 30 to 60 minutes during the day that is 100 percent mine with no interruptions. It's not reasonable or practical to say that every day I'm going to take a jacuzzi or do this or that to relax because schedules are too unpredictable. It is reasonable to look at my schedule and find some time I can block out for myself," she says. "When that time arrives, I choose any activity that appeals to me at the moment— whether it's exercising vigorously, napping briefly, or just letting the thoughts flow freely. This time is the most therapeutic part of my day."

ℬusy Woman's Break

"It's how we spend our time that determines if we are free or if we are in prison," says Marcia Wieder, a self-proclaimed dreams-come-true consultant and author of *Making Your Dreams Come True* and *Life Is but a Dream*. A resident of San Francisco (her dream city), she travels the world to give workshops and speeches on visionary planning, team building, and dream fulfillment.

"If you are living in time-bound awareness, there are things you can do to be in a more natural flow," she suggests. "Explore the realm of timelessness by taking off your watch, turning off the television, meditating, sleeping late, or taking a nap. Timelessness lives in our hearts. It's like being swept away by a beautiful piece of music. In this realm, our lives are experienced differently."

✦ *Your Time Savors* ✦

PART 12

Great Escapes
Getting away from it all

"Send me out into another life. But get me back
for supper."

—*Faith Popcorn*

*To find a great escape, you can call your travel agent or
simply look in your own backyard. From the beaches of
St. Tropez to the hiking trails at a nearby park, regular
breaks are a well-deserved gift to your soul. So pack your
bags! This chapter offers an itinerary of great getaways.*

Get away from the real world—if only for a few hours. Go to a park for a hike, bike ride, or fishing trip and soak in the natural beauty.

✦

Always take vacations. Every year, be sure you take one that's at least a week long. Don't kid yourself by believing your company can't survive without you. You're no good to them if you're burnt out.

Get back to nature at a country resort
or rural B&B.

◆

Stop at a roadside market.

◆

Explore a new city—or even your own—
just after the crack of dawn.

Make the weekends your time to rejuvenate. The key is to maximize your time for enjoyment and minimize your time for obligations.

- ✦ Go to bed early on Friday night.
- ✦ Stop doing chores on Saturday and Sunday. Do small chores every week night.
- ✦ Plan a special activity, like wine tasting, going out to the movies, dinner, or ballroom dancing.
- ✦ Turn off the phones and take a Saturday nap.
- ✦ Consolidate errands and set a time frame for completing them.

*E*very once and a while, take the back roads
to your destination.

✦

Visit one of America's most exciting cities
and do the town.

✦

For a taste of the laid-back lifestyle,
attend a small town fair.

Take in a spectacular view—from sitting on a beach at sunset to gazing at the city from atop the Empire State Building.

✦

Take a travel adventure. Tour companies offer special ways to see beautiful destinations—from mountain climbing and sea kayaking to hiking and horseback riding.

$\mathcal{T}$ake a ride in the country to savor the
fall foliage.

✦

Catch some rays and read a book on one
of your favorite beaches.

✦

Just once, fly first class.

See your tax dollars at work in a way that will make you proud. Visit a national park.

◆

Spend a long weekend in a charming town where there's little to do but relax and take it easy.

$\mathscr{P}$ick up a guide book to prepare for an upcoming trip. Psyche yourself up by reading about the city and its alluring attractions. It's almost as much fun as being there.

◆

For rest and renewal, give yourself a day of R&R each week. Even God took one day off.

Travel safely when you're going solo.

+ Book a trip through a women-friendly operation or women's tour group.
+ Never put your home phone number on your baggage tags.
+ Carry your luggage onto the plane, if possible.
+ Stay at bed and breakfast inns instead of hotels.
+ If you're staying at a hotel, don't stay in a room on the ground floor.

*W*hen you go on vacation, leave your work
at the office—no exceptions!

◆

See America. On your next trip, take the train.

◆

Don't ever, ever forget to take your camera!

For needed respite, take a day off and tell everyone you're going out of town. Instead, spend the day at home catching up on chores, watching the latest Tom Cruise video, finishing that novel, or baking bread from scratch.

Make a window seat complete with a plush, flowery cushion, bookshelves, and delicate drapes. It's a great destination for reading, journaling, meditating, or taking in the view.

◆

Right now, take out your calendar and block off time within the next six months for vacations, long weekends, and special splurges. By planning ahead, you'll take control of your schedule—instead of vice versa.

Make a list of the places you'd like to see in your lifetime. Set aside $50 each month in an interest-bearing savings account to help you reach your destinations.

◆

Turn business into pleasure. Extend a business trip by a few days to see the sights (instead of just the board rooms) in a fabulous city.

Go off-season.

+ You'll beat the crowds.
+ You can't beat the prices.
+ You'll experience your destination in a whole new light—the beach in the fall, a national park at the first sign of spring, a serene lake in the winter, the ski slopes in July.

ℬusy Woman's Break

Gail Snowden, president of First Community Bank of Boston, is responsible for a network of 52 inner-city neighborhood branches, a community-based lending operation, and two loan production resource centers that serve three states. A resident of Boston, MA, Gail is also active in numerous professional associations and civic and community groups. She serves on the boards of Northeastern University, Businesses for Social Responsibility, and American Student Assistance Group.

To escape from the daily grind, she heads to the sunny shores. "I really enjoy going to the beach. I find the sun, sand, and water to be very renewing and relaxing," says Gail, who also escapes on regular walks to relieve everyday stress.

ℬusy Woman's Break

"I'm a complete workaholic," says Hollywood producer and casting director Katy Wallin, owner of **Katy & Co.**, a casting facility in Burbank, CA. "I started my company at a young age and have been working hard at it ever since. "I love what I do, but I can't enjoy it if my entire life is engulfed by work," Katy says. "I finally realized that balance is important spiritually, mentally, physically, and emotionally. If I'm missing one of those pieces, I'd have a hard time in any job, especially in the entertainment industry. I found out the hard way that if you manifest stress, you become ill. I recently spent a most peaceful weekend in Sedona, AZ—a spiritually rejuvenating place. I stayed in a cabin with no phone, TV, fax, or cellular phone. Sometimes it's necessary to take yourself away from all of those external demands."

Katy's long list of credits includes casting for the mega-popular children's hit, *The Mighty Morphin Power Rangers,* and running the **Women's Image Network,** an organization she co-founded to offer development money to people who create film and television projects that depict women in a positive light. Katy is also producing her first independent film under the banner of **Mystic Art Pictures,** her newly formed production company.

✦ *Your Great Escapes* ✦

PART 13

Soul Food
Creating memorable meals and other treats

"Everything you see I owe to spaghetti."

—*Sophia Loren*

There's nothing like food to evoke a mood—like a cup of hot chocolate to warm your soul or a heaping serving of macaroni and cheese to chase away the blues. But dieters beware! This chapter encourages occasional indulgences and offers a bounty of ideas for savoring mealtime moments.

$\mathcal{E}$njoy a hot-fudge sundae—guilt-free.

◆

Treat yourself to an afternoon tea with friends.

◆

Bake bread from scratch.

Make ordinary meals extraordinary. Serve meatloaf on your finest china. Drink soda from a crystal glass. Wipe your mouth with a cloth napkin. Light a candle.

◆

Don't plan ahead. Go to the market and pick out fresh bread, vegetables, meat, flowers, wine, coffee, and dessert for a spectacular, spontaneous meal.

Make a hot toddy and enjoy it in front of a fire you made yourself.

✦

Make a batch of chocolate chip cookies and eat them warm with a glass of cold milk.

$\mathscr{E}$njoy a treat that evokes positive memories from your childhood.

- ✦ Eat Oreos cream-first.
- ✦ Toast marshmallows.
- ✦ Pack a PB&J for lunch.
- ✦ Make s'mores.
- ✦ Eat cookie dough.

Spice up your brown bag lunches. Forget the mushy microwave pizza. Instead, pack a few slices of french bread, gouda cheese, and honey mustard. Or substitute kiwi or mango for ordinary apples and oranges. Even a special spread, like chutney or spicy mustard, can liven up the simplest sandwich.

$\mathcal{B}$uy one really good cookbook that you can refer to for a good recipe in any situation. Get cookin' with these volumes:

- *The Silver Palate Cookbook* by Julie Russo and Sheila Lukins.
- *Martha Stewart Anthology Cookbook* by Martha Stewart.
- *Southern Living Cookbook* published by Oxmoor House.
- *The Joy of Cooking* by Irma S. Rombauer and Marion Rombauer Becker.
- *Better Homes and Gardens New Cook Book* by the Better Homes and Gardens Test Kitchen.

$\mathscr{H}$ave breakfast for dinner. I remember when my dad would make pancakes as big as the skillet. It was one of our favorite family meals.

◆

Make a homemade vanilla milkshake and sip it with a straw.

$\mathscr{E}$njoy a glass of wine with your evening meal. Your local wine store can help you make a good selection that pleases your palate and your pocketbook.

◆

Splurge at the movies by sprinkling M&Ms into a tub of hot, buttered popcorn.

*P*ut your famous family recipes into a "homemade" recipe book. Give them to family members, to be handed down from generation to generation.

◆

Add sweet, spicy flavor to everyday foods. Keep a mixture of cinnamon sugar handy to sprinkle on toast, popcorn, ice cream, or hot or cold cereal.

*U*se fresh herbs instead of dried.

◆

Say a word of thanks before every meal.

◆

Try a new restaurant.

Set the mood before your guests arrive.

+ Pre-program your CD player with a variety of songs that will add a soothing backdrop to the evening.
+ Dim the lights and light candles throughout the house, including one in the bathroom.
+ Set out a cold hors d'oeuvre for early arrivals.
+ Make a special welcome sign for the door.
+ Put place cards on the table.
+ Arrange furniture so it maximizes comfort and encourages conversation.

$\mathscr{R}$elax the southern way with a refreshing glass of sweet iced tea. The recipe's easy: Fill a large saucepan with five cups of cold water. Add 1 1/4 cup of sugar, and bring to a boil, stirring occasionally. Remove from heat. Add eight tea bags and steep for eight minutes. Pour tea into a gallon-size pitcher filled 3/4 full with ice. Enjoy!

$\mathcal{L}$iven up dinner parties for you and your guests by creating a catchy theme.

+ Usher in summer with a "Back-to-the-Beach" buffet. Place seashells in decorative patterns around your entrees. Drape a beach towel over the chairs. Serve a trifle for dessert out of a sand bucket. And, of course, embellish all drinks with a little umbrella.

+ Celebrate the "Old West." Eat outside on the picnic table. Make placemats and napkins out of bandanas. Serve western-inspired food, like barbecued ribs, baked beans, and cole slaw. Encourage everyone to come in casual, country digs.

+ Have a "Doodle of a Dinner." Cover the table with a plain paper tablecloth. Create a centerpiece out of a large box of Crayola crayons and distribute a few beside each plate. They'll encourage your guests to interact with each other by playing tic-tac-toe, writing special messages, doodling, or striking up a game of Pictionary.

$\mathscr{G}$o out to breakfast on a workday. Take a friend or plan your day's to-do list over coffee.

◆

At the first sign of summertime, fire up the grill and throw on some burgers topped with muenster cheese. Add fresh ears of corn wrapped in foil. Serve with a juicy slice of watermelon.

ℬusy Woman's Break

"In my job and at home, I constantly have people calling on me," says single mom Theresa Nelson-Page, director of corporate communications for the **Jenkins Group,** a small press book publishing consultant group in Traverse City, MI. "When I have the chance, I like to go out to a cafe and get a cup of coffee and a croissant and become one of everybody else. It's quiet because it's just me. I'm alone amongst a crowd. That centers me and brings me back to earth."

*B*usy Woman's Break

Food is arguably the biggest part of Donna Kunz's life. As a senior account manager in **McCormick's Flavor Division,** she calls on clients including Mars, Cadbury Beverages, Pepperidge Farm, and Kraft. Being around food that often might turn other people away from shameless snacking, but not Donna. Food even figures into her favorite stress busting activity. She admits, "Eating chocolate is always a beautiful experience. I would say that, for a brief moment, it makes me feel better." Donna lives in Connecticut with her husband, and (not so coincidentally) a chocolate lab named Truffles.

✦ *Your Soul Food* ✦

PART 14

Family Matters
Strengthening the ties that bind

"Call it a clan, call it a network, call it a tribe, call it a family. Whatever you call it, whoever you are, you need one."

—*Jane Howard*

Having it all doesn't just mean working in a high-powered career, driving a fancy car, and owning a big house. As a woman, you have the power to make your biggest contribution through your family—as a loving mother, daughter, sister, or spouse. You can have it all by establishing meaningful traditions, nurturing a sense of closeness and creating an environment full of family fun.

227

$\mathcal{B}$ring the kids into the kitchen. Have them help toss the salad, pack lunches, or set the table.

◆

Teach tradition and responsibility. Hand down something personal and precious to a younger member of the family.

*I*nvolve your children in charity work. Encourage them to join a scouting or church group or donate a toy to needy children.

◆

Leave work at the office—literally and emotionally. I can't undervalue the importance of this gesture to you and your family.

Give lots of hugs—literally, but also figuratively.

- ✦ Praise even the smallest accomplishments.
- ✦ Tell your family you love them—often.
- ✦ Leave cards or small tokens of affection in book bags and briefcases.
- ✦ Be there to listen and offer support in times of need.
- ✦ Kiss a boo-boo.

$\mathcal{P}$lan a summer picnic at a state park.

✦

Call your mother—two days in a row.

✦

Read, read, read to your children.

$\mathcal{F}$ill the holiday season with wonder and fun.

- Take the whole family to a local farm to select and cut down your Christmas tree.
- Go caroling.
- Write clues on your presents.
- Gather around the fire with a cup of hot chocolate or spiced cider and share traditional holiday stories.
- Ask everyone to help plan and prepare the holiday meal.
- Drive or walk around your neighborhood to look at decorations.
- Create holiday traditions your family will look forward to every year. Involve everyone in the planning.

$\mathcal{M}$ake every family birthday a special
event—complete with decorations, gifts, cake,
and a meal chosen by the birthday boy or girl.

✦

Eat dinner together as often as possible. Use
this special time to have meaningful conversation and catch up on the day's activities.

$\mathcal{S}$chedule individual dates with your children. It will make them feel special and allow you to get to know each other a little bit better.

◆

Plant a tree in your backyard or in a park. It will be a symbol of your family's love and growth. Perhaps your grandchildren will picnic under it someday.

*E*ncourage family play with games like
Monopoly, Life, and charades.

✦

Play with your children in a pile of leaves.

✦

Teach your children something new every day.

$\mathcal{O}$rganize your clean-up team. Regularly schedule a "chore day," when each family member is assigned a different task to spruce up your home.

◆

Keep a master calendar in the kitchen so you can keep track of each other's schedules—and plan time for special family activities.

$\mathscr{P}$ut the fun back in family vacations.

+ Have your children help choose a
  destination and plan the trip. The
  Internet is a great place to start your
  research and planning—and a great
  opportunity for learning.

+ Develop a point system for activities
  that allows everyone to do something
  they enjoy while, at the same time,
  teaches them to appreciate the interests
  of others. Give each family member one
  point for the most fantastic thing they
  want to do on the trip. All family
  members take part in each activity.

+ Encourage your children to bring home
  a special memento from each destination—from a T-shirt to a seashell.

Ask your children about their dreams and wishes for the future. Let them know that anything is possible.

◆

Host a family karaoke night—either at your own home or a local club. It will give your "stars" encouragement to shine.

Research your family tree.

◆

Plan a family reunion.

◆

Pitch a tent and camp out with the kids
in your backyard.

Have an "open door" policy with your children. Make it safe for them to discuss difficult issues. This will plant the seeds of openness, honesty, and trust.

◆

Create a "Wall of Fame" in your family room where everyone can display their accomplishments—from a straight-A report card to the latest sketch from art class.

Let your children explore different activities, hobbies, and skills. The more you expose them to, the more they will appreciate, learn, and enjoy.

◆

If you want to be a role model for your children, set a good example. Give them something great to emulate.

Busy Woman's Break

As president and CEO of **Lifedesigns,** Gail Blanke spearheads a company whose vision is to empower women worldwide to design truly exceptional lives. Formerly an executive at Avon, she is an award-winning business woman, internationally known speaker, and co-author of *Taking Control of Your Life: The Secrets of Successful Enterprising Women.* Gail stays in tune with the needs of busy women by serving as president of the New York Chapter of the Women's Forum, as corporate director of The Fonda Group, Inc., and as a board member of several other women's organizations. She is currently at work on the book version of the Lifedesigns Basic Workshop.

A wife and mother, Gail savors quiet family moments in her New York City home. She explains, "My favorite way to relax is to sit in our hot tub with my two wonderful daughters, sip a very cold glass of white wine, and listen to Pavarotti."

$\mathcal{B}$usy Woman's Break

"In the most general sense, my philosophy for maintaining a healthy balance in my life can be summed up in one word: choices," proclaims Frances Hughes Glendening, First Lady of the State of Maryland and executive assistant and chief legal and policy advisor to one of the six commissioners at the Federal Election Commission.

"I have made choices about my life and focus my time and effort in those areas so my behavior comports with my values. I have made my family my number-one priority, reserving 'family time' on our calendars weeks, sometimes months, ahead. Second, I chose the organizations where I would channel my energies. My personal experiences have prompted me to become involved with hospice, suicide prevention, the arts, women's history and women's issues, and preventing violence among our youth. Third, I decided to make time for myself and to spend quality time with friends. Finally, I made the choice to live a healthy life. I exercise regularly and choose to eat vegetarian and low-fat meals."

The First Lady and her husband, Parris, Maryland's 59th Governor, live in University Park with their teenage son, Raymond. One of her many current projects is a book that spotlights women of achievement in Maryland history.

✦ Your Family Matters ✦

PART 15

Homey Comforts
Making your house a home

"A house is no home unless it contains food and fire
for the mind as well as for the body."

—*Margaret Fuller*

*The home is where the heart is, so the saying goes. To
bring more "heart" into your home, these ideas offer ways
to add those personal touches that make your home a true
reflection of your personality and taste. They'll help you
create a welcome respite on your little part of the planet.*

*C*reate a cozy reading nook near a window or fireplace—complete with a big, comfortable chair, warm blanket, end table, tea cozy, and reading lamp.

◆

Buy beautiful, comfortable linens that beckon you to sleep, nap, read a good book, or take a roll in the hay.

Turn ordinary doorways into grand entrances.

+ Make or buy a stunning wreath to put on your front door at the change of every season.
+ Place decorative trees or flower pots on both sides of the door.
+ Buy colorful, functional doormats to place inside and outside each door.
+ Dress up an old door with a fresh coat of colored paint and a bright brass doorknob, door knocker, kick-plate, and mail slot.

*P*lant a garden. The variety of flowers and vegetables available allow you to design a colorful masterpiece that fits your taste and time constraints.

◆

Beckon nature's creatures to your backyard. Hang a birdhouse or plant a butterfly garden.

Add sparkle to a room by hanging a
colorful sun catcher in the window.

✦

Buy a piece of junk and turn it
into a treasure.

✦

Light a fire in the fireplace and
play some classical music.

249

$\mathcal{F}$ill your home with wonderful scents. You have endless options.

- Mix a little vanilla extract with water and simmer on the stove.
- Set out fresh potpourri in a big ceramic bowl. Replace frequently with new scents that reflect the season.
- Light a scented candle.
- Sprinkle scented crystals into the vacuum bag before you clean.
- Make a great-smelling dish—chocolate chip cookies, fresh bread, or chicken soup.
- Put floral-scented sachets in drawers and closets, or line the drawers and shelves with scented paper.

*I*nstead of buying new furniture, rearrange what you already have—or update your look with smaller touches, like new throw pillows, stenciling, lamps, pictures, slip covers, or knick-knacks.

◆

Decorate every room in your house so that something beautiful is always in sight— whether it's a vase of fresh flowers, a favorite antique, or a treasured family photo.

 ring a bit of sunshine into winter days.

- ✦ Make lemonade from scratch.
- ✦ Force bulbs to yield fragrant hyacinth or elegant paper whites.
- ✦ Plant an indoor herb garden.
- ✦ Make a seashell lamp.
- ✦ Buy a bunch of sunflowers to put in a big vase on the dining room table.

$\mathcal{B}$uy coffee table books to display and
peruse as the mood strikes.

✦

Splurge on a great piece of art that speaks
to your soul.

✦

Have your windows and carpets
professionally cleaned once a year.

*P*ut a window box outside your kitchen window and fill it with seasonal flowers: daffodils for spring, geraniums for summer, mums for fall, and evergreens for winter.

✦

Declare a "stress-free zone"—the living room couch, your bed, or the bathtub. Escape to this place whenever you need to slow down, chill out, or put things in proper perspective. Keep treats close at hand—a romance novel, chocolates, or a lavender-scented eye pillow.

Make small changes in your decor to suit the season. Lampshades, bed linens, towels, potpourri, flowers, and slipcovers can help you create a new look.

◆

In warm weather, expand your home to the great outdoors. Buy a big umbrella and table set for dining on the deck, a swing for lounging the porch, or an Adirondack chair for reading under a backyard tree.

$\mathcal{I}$f you must bring the office home, designate a special work space in your family room or extra bedroom. The area should include a desk and all the other supplies necessary to get the job done. Remind your children and your spouse, that when you are sitting there, it means "Do Not Disturb." And make a promise to yourself and your family that you won't spread your work to other areas of the house.

Treat weekend visitors like VIPs with a guest room and special touches reminiscent of the finest B&Bs:

- Hang fluffy bath towels and washcloths over a chair in the bedroom.
- Put crisp, fresh linens on the bed right before they arrive.
- Put a vase of fresh flowers on the dresser.
- Hang two terry cloth robes on the back of the door.
- Stock bedside tables with a variety of books and magazines.
- Sneak in the room in the evening to turn down the covers and put chocolates on the pillows.
- Slip the newspaper under the door on Sunday morning.
- Bake fresh muffins for breakfast and serve with cafe au lait.

ℬusy Woman's Break

Nationally known motivational speaker Donna Tyson compares her life to a sponge. "In order for me to give energy, peace, and wisdom to others, I must fill myself back up every now and then. To do that, I literally create a mini-oasis in my home that nurtures my spirit and my brain and allows me to slow down," she says. "I put on soft music, light candles, brew aromatic coffee, and sit in front of a window to take in the light and the view. I savor the moment by taking deep breaths and letting my senses feast on the pleasant sensations I've created around me."

Donna is president of **D.R. Tyson Management, Inc.** based in Fredericksburg, VA. She is the single mother of three teenagers who serve as the inspiration for many of her unforgettable stories.

*B*usy Woman's Break

As a military spouse who has moved every one to two years of her adult life, Kathie Hightower has had to deal with constant change and personal upheaval. "Because I move so much, I've learned to quickly make a home my own. Your home is such a haven, it's important to make it right for you," she explains. "Simple things work wonders for me, like putting on great music while I'm working, using aromatic candles and oils, filling rooms with color and playful things, and eating dinner by candlelight—even if we're having leftovers."

A writer and motivational speaker, Kathie shares these unique suggestions with audiences around the world through seminars and in her booklet, *Joyful Living*. She is owner of Hightower Resources and serves as a Lieutenant Colonel in the U.S. Army Reserve. Her current home base is in Corvallis, OR.

✦ Your Homey Comforts ✦

PART 16

Daily Diversions
Taking time to unwind

"Millions long for immortality who do not know what
to do with themselves on a rainy Sunday afternoon."
—*Susan Ertz*

*Tied up in the demands of your daily life? Step out of the
whirlwind and unwind with these novel ideas for
uncommonly good fun.*

$\mathcal{T}$reat yourself. Go to the mall and buy something that is distinctly you, but that you've never had the nerve to get—a lace teddy, a cashmere sweater, expensive perfume, a cappuccino maker, or rollerblades.

◆

Make a list of the great books you've always wanted to read. Go to the library and check out the first one. Read and return it by the due date, and cross it off the list. Repeat.

Watch a classic movie. It's true they just don't make them like that anymore.

◆

Search for seashells on the beach and make something with the ones you find.

◆

Play air guitar to your favorite music— no holds barred.

$\mathcal{B}$rowse through a bookstore with no titles in mind, and buy something that intrigues you.

✦

Tape episodes of your favorite sitcom. Keep them in your video library for times when you need a boost.

$\mathcal{L}$ose yourself in a great mystery or suspense novel—one you won't want to put down until you're finished.

◆

Make an audiotape of songs that most inspire you. Listening to it is a great way to lift your spirits.

$\mathcal{P}$op popcorn and rent a video that speaks to your mood. It's one of my favorite diversions. Movies can absorb you and take you to another time and place. I've listed the ones I turn to again and again for romance, excitement, inspiration, and just plain, old fun.

◆

Get swept away by a great romance video:

- *The Prince of Tides* starring Barbra Streisand and Nick Nolte
- *An Affair to Remember* starring Deborah Kerr and Cary Grant
- *To Dance with the White Dog* starring Jessica Tandy and Hume Cronin
- *Casablanca* starring Humphrey Bogart and Ingrid Bergman
- *When Harry Met Sally* starring Meg Ryan and Billy Crystal
- *Say Anything* starring John Cusack and Ione Skye

$\mathscr{B}$e exhilarated by an edge-of-your-seat thriller or horror video:

- *The Terminator* series starring Arnold Schwarzenegger
- *Alien* starring Sigourney Weaver
- *Nightmare on Elm Street* (the original) starring Robert Englund
- *Halloween* (the original) starring Jamie Lee Curtis
- *The Fugitive* starring Harrison Ford
- *Silence of the Lamb*s starring Jodie Foster and Anthony Hopkins
- *Raiders of the Lost Ark* starring Harrison Ford

Savor a good cry with these three-hanky videos:

- *Terms of Endearment* starring Debra Winger and Shirley MacLaine
- *Love Story* starring Ali McGraw and Ryan O'Neil
- *Brian's Song* starring James Caan and Billy Dee Williams
- *Steel Magnolias* starring Sally Field and Julia Roberts
- *Phenomenon* starring John Travolta

*B*oost your spirits with a video that will make you stand up and cheer. These are sure to satisfy:

- *It's a Wonderful Life* starring Jimmy Stewart
- *Forrest Gump* starring Tom Hanks
- *Mr. Holland's Opus* starring Richard Dreyfuss
- *Rocky* (the original) starring Sylvester Stallone
- *Star Wars* starring Mark Hamill, Harrison Ford, and Carrie Fisher

Laugh your head off at these classic comedy videos:

- *Tootsie* starring Dustin Hoffman
- *The Philadelphia Story* starring Katherine Hepburn, Cary Grant, and Jimmy Stewart
- *Big* starring Tom Hanks and Elizabeth Perkins
- *Vacation* starring Chevy Chase (sorry, but I really like it)
- *Wayne's World* starring Mike Myers (hey, we're talking laughs here, not cinematography)

$\mathscr{C}$heck out the latest exhibit at the art gallery. (While you're there, buy yourself something special from the gift shop.)

✦

Buy concert tickets to see a group you loved in your younger years—from the Moody Blues or Rolling Stones to The Who or The Monkees. Share your memories by taking along the kids—hey, most of these groups are still "hip."

Sew to your heart's content. A recent study shows that women who sew experience a significant drop in heart rate and blood pressure compared to women who participated in other leisure activities.

◆

Visit your furry friends at the local zoo.

$\mathscr{C}$reate a soothing ritual to transition
yourself from work to home.

- Take three deep breaths before walking
  in the front door.
- The minute you walk in the house, stash
  your briefcase out of sight.
- Sip a cocktail, micro-brewed beer, or
  glass of wine.
- Slip into something more comfortable.
- Open the daily mail.
- Hug your dog.
- Throw your arms up in the air and shout,
  "Yes! I made it through another day!"

$\mathcal{C}$heck out the women on the web with these female-friendly Internet sites:

- **Women's Work** (http://www.wwork.com) and **Women's Wire** (http://www.women.com), on-line magazines that cover issues ranging from getting ahead at work to managing stress.
- **Cybergrrl Webstation** (http://www.cybergrrl.com), a site that introduces women to the wonders of the World Wide Web.
- **WWWomen!** (http://www.women.com), a search-engine for women-related articles.
- **BizWomen** (http://www.bizwomen.com), the place to post your on-line business card or network with other women in your field.

$\mathcal{S}$kip a stone across a pond.

✦

Play a tune on the piano—even if it's
chopsticks.

✦

Subscribe to the magazine you're
always skimming in the store.

*B*usy Woman's Break

Pam Shriver is the consummate overachiever. She burst onto the international tennis scene in 1978 when she reached the U.S. Open final as a 16-year-old amateur. Since then, she has won 21 singles titles and 112 doubles championships, plus the 1988 Olympic Gold Doubles Medal which she shared with Zina Garrison Jackson. Pam has been ranked as high as number three in the world in singles and number one in doubles.

Now a sought-after speaker, this Baltimore native continues to contribute to the world of sports and to her community. Pam is a contributing editor to *Tennis* magazine and an analyst for ABC Sports and ESPN. She is a vice president of the International Tennis Hall of Fame and is on the U.S.T.A. Board of Directors and the International Tennis Federation's Olympic Committee. She also hosts an annual tennis exhibition that benefits local children's charities.

When it's time for Pam to wind down, little escapes help a lot. "I find several fun ways to relax and get away from the pressure scene," she confides. "I enjoy getting an hour or 90-minute massage, going to a good movie, or joining a group of friends for a meal, either home cooked (not at my home!), or at a great restaurant."

ℬusy Woman's Break

A self-described "reformed lawyer," Tina Ravitz is vice president of Technology and Business Operations for media giant **Viacom, Inc.** Even though about half of her time is spent traveling, Tina still finds time for personal diversions. "I try to play tennis at least once a week. It's great. Not only am I getting exercise, I'm also recreating in the truest sense because I'm playing a game. I'm thinking about the strategy, and it totally absorbs my mind and my body," she says. "When my pocketbook can afford it and my body needs it, I also go to a massage therapist. These two activities are the perfect balance of exercise and relaxation."

Tina also takes time to support her alma mater, Princeton University. She serves on the Board of Trustees and the Executive Committee of the Princeton University Press. For the past 18 years, she has been on the board of the American Whig-Cliosophic Society, a political and debating society of which she was the first female president during her undergraduate years.

✦ Your Daily Diversions ✦

Afterword

"Life is about not knowing, having to change, taking the
moment and making the best of it, without knowing
what's going to happen next."

— Gilda Radner

Armed with hundreds of new ideas and the inspiration of wonderful role models, you're now prepared to
savor the joys of being—of discovering the magic
moments that so quietly fill our lives if we just take the
time, look, and listen. By choosing a world full of
magic—rather than one of stress, pressures, and self-
constraints—you'll open yourself up to countless possibilities and long-lasting joy. Making this mental shift
will not be easy, but each small step is as fulfilling as
the ultimate reward.

Take the first step by vowing to give yourself at
least one magic moment every day. You might start with
a quick relaxation technique or by leaving work on time.
You may even realize that your life is already full of
magic moments. The key is to recognize them as such,
instead of taking them for granted.

After you make magic moments part of your daily
routine, you'll find that a funny thing happens. You will
realize that you are in control. You will stop blaming

and start appreciating. You will stop grumbling and start rejoicing. When I simply slow down and look at the wonders of my small, but glorious world—my husband's smile, the unconditional love of my dog, the tree budding in my backyard, the ability to create my own life—I know we are on much more than a physical journey. We are on a quest of the spirit and the soul. Everything around us is somehow connected, and everything within us is a gift that was meant to be shared.

If you're waiting for your "real life" to begin, you're wasting precious time. This truth hit Joyce Wadler only after being diagnosed with breast cancer. Fortunately, she won the fight. On a recent salute to breast cancer survivors on Lifetime Television, actress Meredith Baxter shared a message from Joyce, whom she played in a TV movie. She said, "Death, I now see, may not come when I'm 85 and weary. It'll come whenever it damn well pleases. So when I see something I want, I grab it. If the tulips are particularly yellow, I buy them. I see how lucky I am to have true friends and a loving family, and I make time for them the way I used to make time for work. If someone treats me disrespectfully, I leave. As for this scar on my breast, I'm happy to have it. It's the battle scar over my heart."

Don't wait until tragedy strikes to discover the magic in your life. I don't. In fact, if someone asked me to describe the best time in my life, I would describe today—no matter what day it is. Feeling successful, loving, proud and joyful are not things you should reserve for special occasions or accomplishments. They are things you should savor every day. It's all about making a commitment to yourself and nurturing the many facets of your life. Hopefully, this book has served as an impetus to start you in the right direction. Along the way, when you discover which magic moments work best for you—and as you create your own—please share your experiences with me so I can share them with others. You can reach me at any of the following:

Mail: Ovations Inc., 1543 Cottage Lane,
Baltimore, MD 21286
E-mail: ovation@erols.com
Phone: 410-821-5979
Fax: 410-583-7951

Thank you for accompanying me on this amazing journey. Here's wishing you a lifetime of magic moments!

Kim Goad

279

About the Author

A home-based entrepreneur, Kim Goad wrote most of this book while wearing her pajamas. Her days are sprinkled with many other "magic moments," such as sipping iced tea on her back porch, taking strength training classes at a local gym, singing, shopping, gazing out her office window, and going to the movies (where she always orders butter on her popcorn).

Kim shares her philosophy on life—to actively create and live by your own definition of success—through dynamic keynote presentations and empowering workshops. A member of the National Speakers Association, she brings common-sense wisdom to decidedly chaotic times and encourages women and other audiences to decrease stress, achieve balance in their lives, communicate more effectively and develop a powerful vision for the future. Also an award-winning writer, Kim has penned dozens of articles on wellness and lifestyle issues.

As president of **Ovations Inc.**, a consulting firm that helps people "live a life that wins rave reviews," Kim spreads the *Magic Moments* philosophy to the corporate world through writing and speaking on personal leadership and effectiveness. She works with clients including the Johns Hopkins Health System, Johnson & Johnson Health Care Systems, Clemson University and The Pampered Chef. Through her community involvement, Kim also promotes adult literacy and supports professional women in their quest for growth, success and happiness.

She lives with her husband, Steve, and golden retriever, Gracie, in Baltimore, MD.

Commune-a-Key Publishing and Seminars

Commune-a-Key Publishing & Seminars was established in 1992. Our mission statement, "Communicating Keys to Growth and Empowerment," describes our effort to publish books that inspire and promote personal growth and wellness. Our books and products provide powerful ways to care for, discover and heal ourselves and others.

Our audience includes health care professionals and counselors, caregivers, women, men, people interested in Native American traditions—anyone interested in personal growth, psychology and inspiration. We hope you enjoy this book!

ORDERING INFORMATION

Commune-a-Key Publishing has a variety of books and products. For further information on our books, or if you would like to receive a catalog or be on our mailing list for future products and seminars, please write or call us at the address and phone number listed below.

Our authors are also available for seminars, workshops and lectures. Please call our toll-free number for further information.

Commune-a-Key Publishing
P.O. Box 58637
Salt Lake City, UT 84158

◆

1-800-983-0600